COLDPLAY

THE CD IS PLAYABLE ON ANY CD PLAYER, AND IS ALSO ENHANCED SO MAC AND PC USERS
CAN ADJUST THE RECORDING TO ANY TEMPO WITHOUT CHANGING THE PITCH!

Cover photo: Peter Neill – ShootTheSound.com

ISBN: 978-1-4768-1837-5

HAL•LEONARD®
CORPORATION
7777 W. BLUEMOUND RD. P.O. BOX 13819 MILWAUKEE, WI 53213

Visit Hal Leonard Online at
www.halleonard.com

CONTENTS

CLOCKS

TROMBONE

Words and Music by GUY BERRYMAN,
JON BUCKLAND, WILL CHAMPION
and CHRIS MARTIN

IN MY PLACE

TROMBONE

Words and Music by GUY BERRYMAN,
JON BUCKLAND, WILL CHAMPION
and CHRIS MARTIN

EVERY TEARDROP IS A WATERFALL

5/6

TROMBONE

Words and Music by GUY BERRYMAN,
JON BUCKLAND, WILL CHAMPION, CHRIS MARTIN,
PETER ALLEN, ADRIENNE ANDERSON and BRIAN ENO

FIX YOU

 7/8

TROMBONE

Words and Music by GUY BERRYMAN,
JON BUCKLAND, WILL CHAMPION
and CHRIS MARTIN

LOST!

TROMBONE

Words and Music by GUY BERRYMAN,
JON BUCKLAND, WILL CHAMPION
and CHRIS MARTIN

PARADISE

TROMBONE

Words and Music by GUY BERRYMAN,
JON BUCKLAND, WILL CHAMPION,
CHRIS MARTIN and BRIAN ENO

THE SCIENTIST

TROMBONE

Words and Music by GUY BERRYMAN,
JON BUCKLAND, WILL CHAMPION
and CHRIS MARTIN

SPEED OF SOUND

TROMBONE

Words and Music by GUY BERRYMAN,
JON BUCKLAND, WILL CHAMPION
and CHRIS MARTIN

TROUBLE

TROMBONE

Words and Music by GUY BERRYMAN,
JON BUCKLAND, WILL CHAMPION
and CHRIS MARTIN

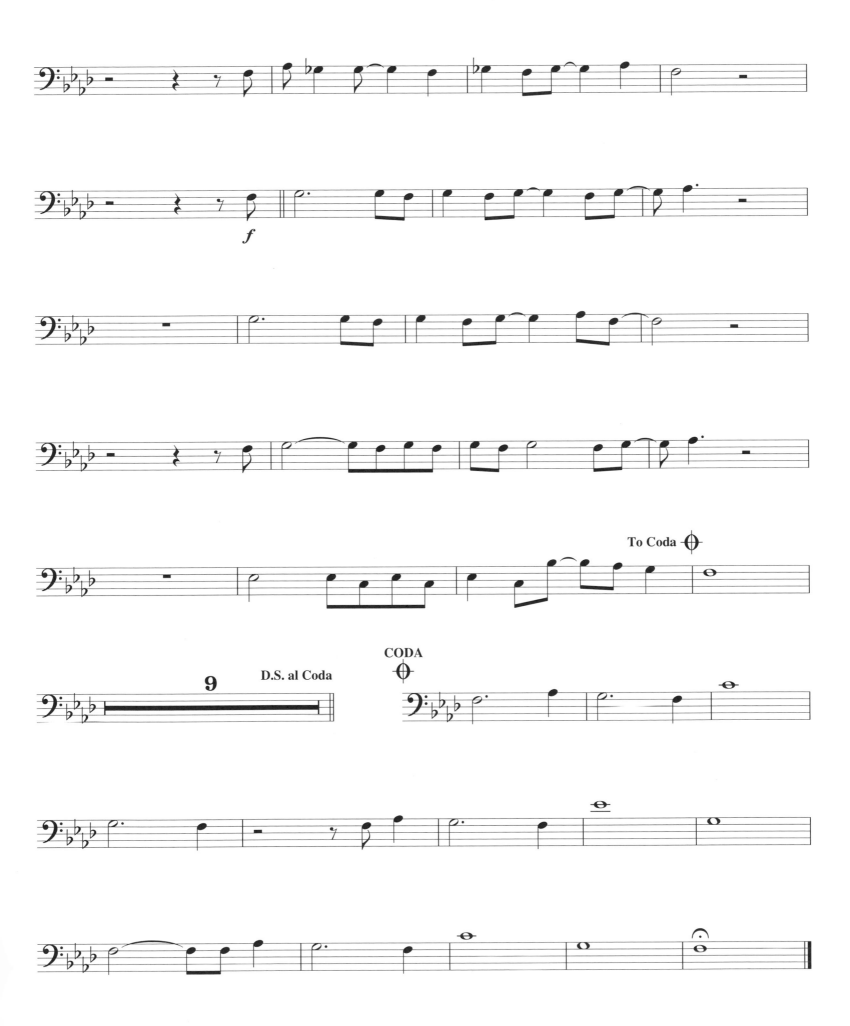

VIOLET HILL

TROMBONE

Words and Music by GUY BERRYMAN,
JON BUCKLAND, WILL CHAMPION
and CHRIS MARTIN

YELLOW

21/22

TROMBONE

Words and Music by GUY BERRYMAN,
JON BUCKLAND, WILL CHAMPION
and CHRIS MARTIN

VIVA LA VIDA

TROMBONE

Words and Music by GUY BERRYMAN,
JON BUCKLAND, WILL CHAMPION
and CHRIS MARTIN

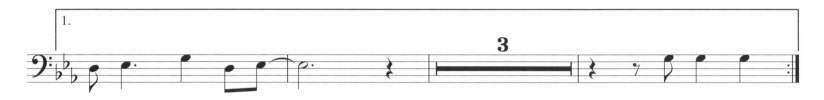

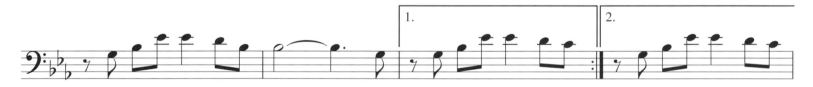